# HAL•LEONARD®

# CELLO
## PLAY-ALONG

AUDIO
ACCESS
INCLUDED

# THE PHANTOM OF THE OPERA

T0055845

## PLAYBACK+
*Speed • Pitch • Balance • Loop*

To access audio visit:
**www.halleonard.com/mylibrary**

Enter Code
**1615-6176-0170-8726**

Trischa Loebl, cello
Audio arrangements by Peter Deneff
Recorded and Produced by Jake Johnson at Paradyme Productions

ISBN 978-1-5400-2509-8

Visit Hal Leonard Online at
**www.halleonard.com**

Contact Us:
**Hal Leonard**
7777 West Bluemound Road
Milwaukee, WI 53213
Email: info@halleonard.com

In Europe contact:
**Hal Leonard Europe Limited**
Distribution Centre, Newmarket Road
Bury St Edmunds, Suffolk, IP33 3YB
Email: info@halleonardeurope.com

In Australia contact:
**Hal Leonard Australia Pty. Ltd.**
4 Lentara Court
Cheltenham, Victoria, 3192 Australia
Email: info@halleonard.com.au

# All I Ask of You

**Music by Andrew Lloyd Webber**
**Lyrics by Charles Hart**
**Additional Lyrics by Richard Stilgoe**

# Think of Me

Music by Andrew Lloyd Webber
Lyrics by Charles Hart
Additional Lyrics by Richard Stilgoe

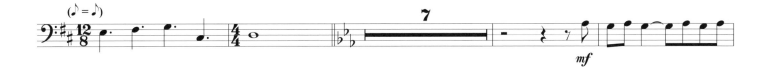

# Angel of Music

**Music by Andrew Lloyd Webber**
**Lyrics by Charles Hart**
**Additional Lyrics by Richard Stilgoe**

# Masquerade

**Music by Andrew Lloyd Webber**
**Lyrics by Charles Hart**
**Additional Lyrics by Richard Stilgoe**

# The Music of the Night

**Music by Andrew Lloyd Webber**
**Lyrics by Charles Hart**
**Additional Lyrics by Richard Stilgoe**

# The Phantom of the Opera

**Music by Andrew Lloyd Webber**
**Lyrics by Charles Hart**
**Additional Lyrics by Richard Stilgoe and Mike Batt**

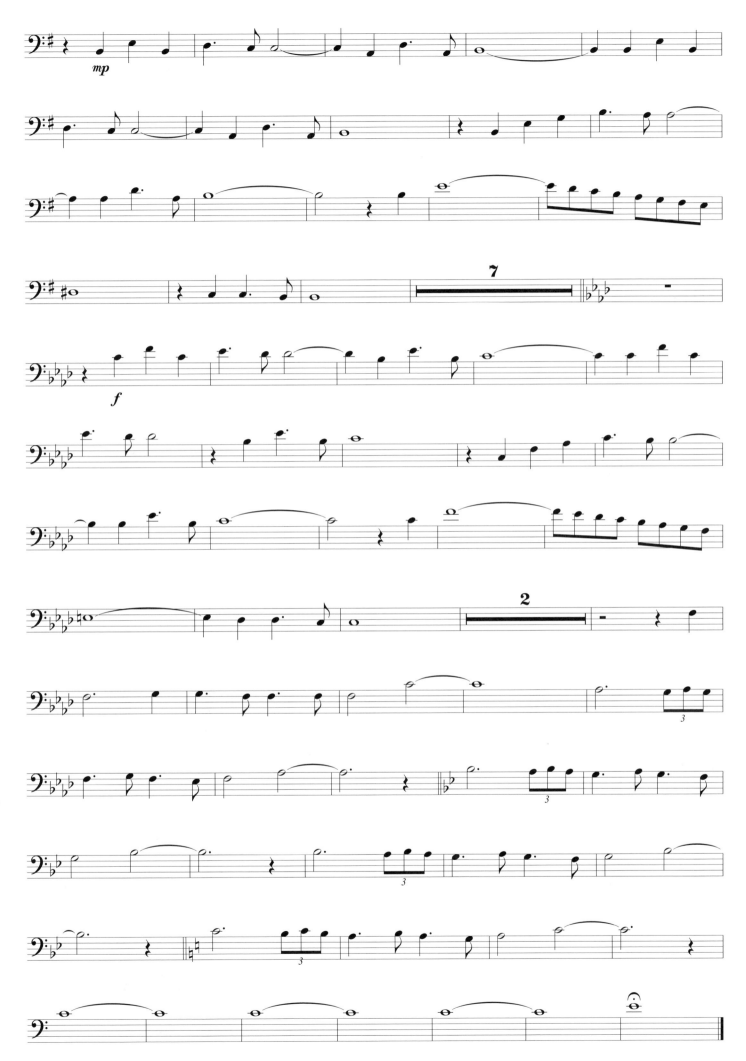

# Wishing You Were Somehow Here Again

**Music by Andrew Lloyd Webber**
**Lyrics by Charles Hart**
**Additional Lyrics by Richard Stilgoe**

# The Point of No Return

**Music by Andrew Lloyd Webber**
**Lyrics by Charles Hart**
**Additional Lyrics by Richard Stilgoe**

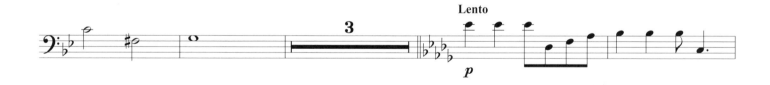